THE
PICNIC BASKET
COOK BOOK
Recipes for Food & Fun!

GOLDEN
WEST ☼
PUBLISHERS

Printed in the United States of America
2nd Printing © 2008

ISBN13: 978-1-58581-025-3
ISBN10: 1-58581-025-8

Information in this book is deemed to be authentic and accurate by the
publisher. However, they disclaim any liability incurred in connection
with the use of information appearing in this book.

Golden West Publishers
4113 N. Longview Ave.
Phoenix, AZ 85014, USA
(602)265-4392
(800)658-5830

For free sample recipes for every Golden West cookbook,
visit: www.goldenwestpublishers.com

Table of Contents

****

Table of Contents

Table of Contents

★★

Introduction

****

*W*hat inspires us to sweep our meals out of the doldrums? It's our yearning for the spice of life, our love for companionship and the sweet kiss of nature, and our desire to feel unfettered and free!

This special cookbook is here to help you do just that. It comes packed with some simple suggestions and a healthy slice of creative ideas. Any time two or more gather for fun and good food can be transformed into a grand adventure!

So don't set the table! Pack the picnic basket! Whether you're looking for a no-fuss impromptu meal to take to the park, an elegant champagne breakfast in the gazebo, or a barbeque feast at the beach, let us help you create the most idyllic and delicious picnics you've ever prepared!

In a country with a hefty choice of fast food restaurants, the art of picnicking risks being lost in default to fast-forward motion. However, preparing to picnic doesn't have to be time-consuming. From picnics that reward a lengthy hike to that quick bite in a public park, meals can be planned ahead or tossed quickly from leftovers in the fridge. If a meal takes a little longer to prepare or eat, remember, this means you get to have more special moments in the great outdoors! After all, you're not in a hurry—you're on a picnic!

The recipes in this book range from no-fuss simple foods to banquet-worthy meals. We offer each one with encouragement that it will inspire you to choose an alternative to the artificial lighting and stuffy air of restaurants or fast food outlets. Whether it is your twenty-minute lunch break, a romantic get-away, or a grand family gathering, there are recipes here for you.

Our serving suggestion: Garnish each dish with a little bit of sun and a lot of fresh air!

Picnic 101

****

$\mathcal{T}$he Great American Get-away

The picnic knows no boundaries of place, season, or time of day. From backyard to mountain meadow, summer to spring, early morning to midnight, the picnic can serve up a meal to nurture and delight.

$\mathcal{W}$here do we gather? Focused on a mission for fun, we head for the....

Beach
Neighborhood Park
River, Lake or Stream
Pool
Campground
Hiking Trail
National Park
Rooftop
Sports Event
Parking Lot
Backyard

$\mathcal{W}$hy do we gather? With very little need for a reason, we pack those baskets for...

Potlucks
Birthday Parties
Tailgate Parties
Church Box Socials
Outdoor Concerts
Fundraisers
Afternoon Teas
Neighborhood Block Parties
Reunions
Anniversary Celebrations
Leaf-Raking and Painting Parties
Romantic Interludes

Picnic 101

****

*W*hen do we gather? We are a hearty nation of fun and joy-seekers who will escape our routines…

     At sunset or sunrise

     As early in spring as we possibly can

     As late in fall as the chill will allow

     Before the desert heat sets in

     After the heat has given up its grip

     When families gather

     When the night is young and hearts are entwined

     On those TGIF nights

     On lunch breaks

     On summer evenings

     On Father's Day

     On Valentine's Day

     On the 4th of July

     On President's Day

     On Mother's Day

     On Memorial Day

     On Labor Day

     On Cinco De Mayo

Picnic 101

★★

*T*he Basket

*W*e all have to have something to carry those yummy vittles in, now don't we?

This traditional Dorothy-style basket is perfect for that romantic picnic for two. It is big enough for food and drinks for you both, but also small enough to carry on your post-picnic stroll.

This backpack-style basket is perfect for the more adventurous picnicker who will be enjoying a well-earned feast after a lengthy walk or hike. It is also good for you organized ones who like the look of matching cutlery, plates, napkins and a picnic blanket! Romance fits in well with this one too!

For those of you planning a large family picnic, an alternative "box" basket is perfect! All you need is one large, sturdy box, a collection of paints, glitter glues, felt-tip pens and stickers and some enthusiastic children. Let them decorate the box however they wish and voila! You have your own made-to-order picnic basket!

If your picnic is a last minute thing, and you don't have any of the above, a canvas tote bag is easily converted into a nifty picnic basket. Its generous

Picnic 101

★★★

size means that you can stock up on food and its canvas material makes it great for keeping sand out of your food on beach picnics.

For any picnic of duration, and a menu of recipes needing to be kept cool, the ice cooler is a must. Of course, not everything goes into the cooler, so one of the above baskets will probably be needed also.

*Y*our Kitchen Away-From-Home

From the fanciest feast to the most casual of picnics, your dining experience can be picture-perfect. Why sit on the dirt, fighting with the bugs over who gets to eat your soggy sandwich off a paper plate, when a little extra planning will offer you a far more languid and enjoyable experience? By using even just a few of the checklist items below, you can transform a quick outdoor bite into a luxurious meal.

BLANKET

Whatever you do, don't forget the blanket! Any blanket or table cloth will allow you to dine in comfort, protected from grit, bumps and pesky creepy crawlers. You may also want to cover the picnic table in the park that still wears spills from its last picnickers. If your linen closet doesn't have what you need, look for fun, inexpensive sheets at a local department store or thrift shop.

Picnic 101

POCKETKNIFE

A pocketknife is a great investment for you serial picknickers. Most often it will include a can opener, scissors, corkscrew and a selection of knives. When armed with one of these, you can handle any food or drink that needs slicing, peeling, trimming or prying open. Your breads, cheeses, fruits and vegetables will serve up fresher and tastier when you slice them on site.

UTENSILS

Paper plates may offer your picnic a party feel, but for a few dollars more, sturdy plastic plates become a great re-usable option. Party shops offer decorative selections of plastic plates, cups and cutlery. Plastic plates can also double as cutting boards and serving platters. Another eco-friendly option is to finally reuse any plastic utensils that have been building up in your kitchen drawers.

CONDIMENTS

For perfect picnic-sized condiments, save up extra packets from fast food outlets. Their single servings of salt and pepper, ketchup, mustard, mayonnaise and relish will take up less space in your basket.

THERMOS

If you can't survive the day without your coffee or tea, a thermos is the only way to go. To get into the summer mood, it can also be filled with homemade lemonade, fruit punch, or even ice cream, all of which will stay cold the entire day!

CAMERA

Whether you're on a romantic picnic for two or a family gathering, a camera will let you preserve those special memories for a lifetime. Disposable cameras usually take a decent photo and can be passed around so that even the kids can become photographers.

Picnic 101

★★

UMBRELLA
No matter how optimistic you may be, packing a small umbrella will never hurt. Remember, the weatherman is often wrong, so that umbrella will be appreciated when you and your basket avoid the surprise downpour.

CHAIRS AND TABLE
For those of you who like outdoor dining but prefer the luxury of being on a restaurant patio, a set of foldaway chairs and table will be a worthwhile investment. A good set can last a lifetime.

FIRST AID
A first aid kit is also a wise item to bring on outings. Kits of all sizes are available at drug stores, but at the very least, pack band aids, antiseptic wipes and gauze bandages. If you are concerned about allergies, some anti-itch cream and antihistamine tablets would be useful also.

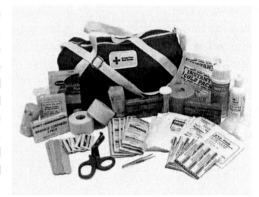

CLEAN-UP ITEMS
Handi-wipes are a must for cleaning up sticky fingers and table surfaces. For a homemade variety, soak napkins in lemon juice and pass around to guests. Pack at least one garbage bag to hold all the leftover trash so that your picnic does not leave a messy mark on your chosen spot in nature. Remember, if you can pack the heavy stuff in, you can tote the lighter stuff out.

The Safety Zone

★★

*W*hen our treasured photos come back from the developer, or are downloaded onto the computer, we all wish for them to be associated with one whopping good time. Cuts and bruises, bug bites, sunburns, wet clothes, food gone bad and lost children are not experiences we want to see as part of our picnic memories. Of course, life can be unpredictable, so heading out with a little preparation is a proactive plus.

To accompany this culinary guide to the perfect picnic, we have collected a few safety and food-preparation ideas worth considering as you plan for a time to remember. Some things can be kept at-ready in your vehicle or even in your basket from one picnic to the next.

Safety

Depending on where you live and how extended your picnic, pack a small survival package that contains at least some of these things:

- First aid kit
    (bandages, antiseptic cream,
    antihistamines etc.)
- Sun block
- Citronella candles
- Whistle
- Snake bite kit
- Small tarp
- Extra blanket or old sleeping bag
- Bug spray
- Umbrella
- Matches
- Water jugs
- Toilet paper and paper towels
- Plastic trash bags
- Water

Surf the Internet for information on buying first aid kits, life jackets, tables, baskets, coolers and camping grills.

Make clear agreements with the kids ahead of time to stay close and observe water safety rules.

The Safety Zone

★★★

Wise Food Preparation

You may be able to see the ants ahead of time and choose a suitable picnic spot, but it's not possible to see, taste or smell dangerous bacteria that can cause illness if food is mishandled. Bacteria grow and multiply rapidly in a danger zone between 40 degrees F and 140 degrees F. Food transported without an adequate ice source or left out in the sun at a picnic won't stay safe for long. Be particularly careful with meats and mayonnaise. Family and friends who eat mishandled food may suddenly get hit with flu-like symptoms that are truly no fun and will surely ruin any picnic.

Follow these tips for preparing and packing food safely for a picnic:

- Some dishes will need to be prepared 1 to 2 days ahead of time. Make sure they are kept cold until time to pack and go.

- Pack those dishes that need to be cold for cooler transport in water-proof containers.

- If possible, try not to take too much extra food to avoid leftovers.

- Clean preparation is essential. Wash hands and work areas. Be sure all utensils are clean before preparing food.

- Foods cooked in advance should be allowed plenty of time to chill thoroughly in the refrigerator. Use an insulated cooler with sufficient ice or ice packs to keep the food at 40 degrees F. Pack food from the refrigerator directly into the cooler.

- If you are planning on take-out foods such as fried chicken or barbequed beef, eat them within two hours of pick-up or buy ahead of time and chill before packing the foods into the cooler.

- Double-wrap raw meat packages, or place in plastic bags and pack in a cooler separately from ready-to-eat foods to prevent cross-contamination.

The Safety Zone

****

- In warm weather, do not put the cooler in the trunk. Carry it inside your air-conditioned car.

- At the picnic, try to store the cooler in the shade. Keep the lid closed and avoid repeated openings. Replenish the ice if it melts.

- Use a separate cooler for drinks so the one containing perishable food will not be constantly opened and closed.

- When handling raw meat, remove from the cooler only the amount that will fit on the grill. The U.S. Department of Agriculture recommends against eating raw or under-cooked ground beef since harmful bacteria could be present.

- Do not partially grill extra burgers to use later. Once you begin cooking burgers by any method, cook them until completely done to assure that bacteria are destroyed.

- When taking foods off the grill, put them on a clean plate to avoid cross-contamination. Do not put the cooked items on the same platter that held the raw meat.

- Place leftover foods in the cooler promptly after serving. Any food left outside for more than an hour should be discarded. If there is still ice in the cooler when you get home, the leftovers are okay to eat.

Family & Friends

✯✯✯

When Family & Friends Gather

Large group gatherings can come in all sorts of shapes and sizes, from family reunions to family and friend get-together's, to church or workplace parties. These larger picnics, usually formed around the potluck theme, offer a fun and healthy break from the habit of kitchen cooking without the cost of restaurant 'eating out.' And preparation takes on a whole new dimension when everyone, from the kids to great-grandparents, is included. There's always a recipe that someone can help do!

Games

One of the great benefits of bringing together a large group of people in one place is the opportunity not only to eat good food, but also to play! Weather permitting and a good playing field, games and contests can bring fun and laughter that will last all day and well into the evening. Here are a few you might want to consider when planning your next big group picnic:

Watermelon Seed Spitting Contest
Frisbee
Badminton
3-Legged Race
Sack Race
Horse Shoes
Egg Toss
Tug-Of-War
Softball
Touch Football
Crochet
Volleyball

Family & Friends

★★

*H*oliday Menus

Holidays may well be number one in our reasons to picnic. We offer you a few menu ideas that come from the many wonderful recipes in this book:

4th of July
- Fried Picnic-Style Chicken
- Bean-N-Bacon Bake
- Deviled Eggs
- Chunky Potato Salad
- Three Sherbet Cooler
- Blackberry Lemonade

Easter
- Ham with Tequila
- Aunt Betty's Cole Slaw
- Carrot Salad
- Hobo Beans
- Apple Pie Cheddar Sundae
- Mulled Cranberry-Apple Cider

Labor Day
- Classic Heroes
- Tuna & Veggie Platter
- Fresh Corn Salad
- Grandma Lucille's Cole Slaw
- S'more Brownies
- Summer Sangria
- Citrus Cooler

Family & Friends

Memorial Day
- Short Ribs Hawaiian Style
- Garlic Shrimp
- Grapefruit & Avocado Salad
- Potato Salad a la Pacific
- Lemon Crumb Squares
- Orange Surprise

Mother's Day
- Marinated BBQ Chuck Steak
- Chilled Artichoke Salad
- Black Bean Salad
- Corn Custard
- Chocolate Cheesecake Cups
- Prospector's Cider

Father's Day
- Mighty Bacon Cheeseburgers
- Potato Salad
- Cilantro Salsa and Chips
- Brownies
- Summer Sangria

Valentine's Day—Try an outdoor breakfast, served to your honey with elegance!
- Sweetheart Breakfast Casserole
- Fresh Fruit
- Champagne
- Your best china, silverware, plastic stemware, picnic tablecloth

★★★

Spotlight on Romance

★★★

Finger Foods

Crisped Chips

Make-Your-Own Salsa

California Cheese Dip with Fresh Fruits

Grilled Peppers and Apples

Beef and Spinach Pita Pockets

Jalapeno Delights

Creamy Cheese Log

Picnic Beef Spread

Sunset Chicken Wings

Garlic Shrimp

Bread, Wine and Thou

Wine Pairings

Burgers and Wine

Snacks and Wine

Spotlight on Romance

★★★

*W*hat is that elusive quality that gives us such a sweet sense of romance? The lure of the unknown, the excitement of surprise, the heart-felt joy of feeling special in the eyes of another, and that soft touch of sun, wind and fragrance. Joined together with succulent morsels and perhaps a touch of wine, we have the romantic picnic for two!

Of all the picnics, this one probably requires the most thoughtful preparation to insure that those special moments are not derailed by forgotten food, pesky bugs or a missing blanket or corkscrew. You might be thinking, "I wish my partner was reading this, so they would get the hint and give this to me." You could just leave this page casually open for them to read, accidentally, of course. Or you could create your own romantic interlude to show them the way. Whether your time together has just begun, or is standing the tests of time, the end result may well be the heart that grows fonder and a relationship that flowers.

Now, you could just grab your sweetheart, cruise through the drive-through, and be on your way, but chips and sodas from the mini-mart do not in themselves equate to romance. Food has, since very ancient times (remember the Roman orgies?), been equated with love and attraction. And not just any food will do. What about strawberries dipped in chocolate and fed to each other? Or a soft delicate cheese  spread on French bread served with apple slices and a glass of champagne? Weigh the ambiance: A bag of chips or marinated veggies and homemade dip…soda in a can or a sparkling glass of wine…you get the picture!

So let's get started on preparation for your next grand adventure! Let's put a Spotlight On Your Romance!

Spotlight on Romance

★★

Finger Foods

CRISPED CHIPS

1 1/2 **Corn Tortillas**
Vegetable Cooking Spray

Lightly spray each side of tortillas with vegetable cooking spray; cut into 8 wedges. Arrange on baking sheet. Bake at 400 degrees, 3 minutes on each side or until crisp.

2 Servings

MAKE-YOUR-OWN SALSA

1/4 cup chopped **Red Onions**
2 tbsps. chopped **Green Bell Peppers**
1 1/2 cloves **Garlic**, minced
1 1/2 tsp.s light **Olive Oil**
1 1/2 cups chopped very ripe fresh **Tomatoes**
1/4 tsp. **Oregano**
1 1/2 tbsps. chopped canned **Jalapeno Peppers**
1 1/4 tbsps. natural **Rice Vinegar**
3 tsps. chopped fresh **Cilantro**
3/8 tsp. **Salt**
Pepper, as desired

Microwave onion, green pepper, garlic and oil 1 minute on high, covered. Add tomatoes and oregano; microwave 2 minutes on high. Stir in remaining ingredients. Refrigerate an hour or overnight to blend flavors.

2 Servings.

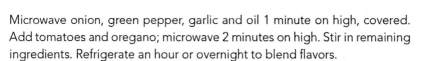

Spotlight on Romance

★★★

CALIFORNIA CHEESE DIP WITH FRESH FRUITS

4 oz. **Cream Cheese**
2 tbsps. **Cream**, or **Milk**
3 tsps. **Honey**
3/4 tsp. **Vanilla**
1/16 tsp. **Nutmeg**, or **Mace**
1/16 tsp. **Cinnamon**
3 tsps. fresh **Lemon Juice**
2 tbsps. diced **Toasted Almonds**

Blend together all ingredients except almonds. Chill. When ready to serve place dip in small bowl. Top with almonds. Place bowl on plate and surround with assorted fruits such as banana slices, melon cubes, grapes, strawberries and peach or nectarine slices.

2 Servings.

GRILLED PEPPERS AND APPLES

2 **Red, Yellow or Green Bell Peppers**
2 **Apples**
1 1/2 tsps. **Oil**
1/4 tsp. **Onion Powder**
1/8 tsp. **Rosemary Leaves**, crushed
1/16 tsp. **Garlic Powder**
1/16 tsp. **Salt**
1/16 tsp. **Black Pepper**

Cut apples and peppers in wedges and toss them with all ingredients. Broil or grill the tossed apples and peppers 15 minutes.

2 Servings.

Spotlight on Romance

★★★

BEEF AND SPINACH PITA POCKETS

8 ounces ground **Beef Top Round**
1 1/2 cloves **Garlic**, minced
1/4 tsp. **Crushed Red Pepper**
1 1/2 cups **Fresh Spinach**, chopped
1/4 tsp. **Ground Cumin**
1/4 tsp. **Ground Coriander**
1/8 tsp. **Ground Ginger**
1/8 tsp. **Salt**
6 fresh **Spinach Leaves**
1 **Whole Wheat Pita Bread**, halved
2 tbsps. **Plain Lowfat Yogurt**
1/8 tsp. **Curry Powder**, (optional)

In large non-stick skillet, combine first 3 ingredients. Cook over medium heat until browned, stirring to crumble beef. Drain in a colander, discard drippings. Wipe skillet dry with a paper towel. Return beef mixture to skillet; add chopped spinach, spices and salt; stir well. Cover and cook over medium heat 3 minutes or just until spinach is wilted; remove from heat. Spoon 1/2 cup beef mixture into each pita half-lined with whole spinach leaves. Mix yogurt with curry powder if desired. Top each pita half with 1 tablespoon yogurt.

Tip: Beef and Spinach Pita Pockets may be individually wrapped and carried in a picnic basket or sack lunch. Keep cool until serving.

2 Servings.

Spotlight on Romance

★★★

JALAPENO DELIGHTS

1 lb. **Sharp Cheddar Cheese**, shredded
1 can (4 oz.) **Jalapenos**, diced
1 medium **Onion**, chopped
3 cloves **Garlic**
1/2 cup **Mayonnaise**
1 cup chopped **Pine Nuts**
Tortilla Chips

Combine cheese, jalapenos, onion and garlic in blender. Add mayonnaise and blend until smooth. Chill until firm. Form into one large ball or 16-20 bite-size balls. Chill until cheese balls are firm. Remove from refrigerator and roll in nuts. Return to refrigerator until ready to serve with your favorite tortilla chips.

CREAMY CHEESE LOG

1 package (8 oz.) **Processed Cheese**, softened
1 package (3 oz.) **Cream Cheese**, softened
1/4 tsp. **Garlic Powder**
1 tbsp. **Lemon Juice**
Ground Red Pepper, to taste
1 tsp. **Paprika**
Chips

Blend processed cheese and cream cheese together in mixing bowl. Add garlic powder, lemon juice and red pepper and blend until fluffy. Place in refrigerator for about 1 hour. When firm, remove and roll into a log shape. Sprinkle paprika over the log and refrigerate again until ready to serve with your favorite chips.

Spotlight on Romance

PICNIC BEEF SPREAD

1 package (8 oz.) **Cream Cheese**, softened
2-3 **Scallions**, chopped
1 small jar **Chipped Beef**, diced
Cayenne Pepper, to taste

Mix all ingredients together in bowl. Shape into a ball with plastic wrap and place in refrigerator overnight. When ready to serve, remove and allow to stand at room temperature until softened. Serve with your favorite tortilla chips.

SUNSET CHICKEN WINGS

1 lb. **Chicken Wings**

Marinade:
1 cup **Soy Sauce**
1 1/3 cups **Brown Sugar**
3/4 cup **Water**
1/4 tsp. **Garlic Powder**
Paprika, to taste

Rinse chicken wings, pat dry and place in pan. Mix together soy sauce, brown sugar, water, and garlic powder. Add soy mixture to chicken, cover, and marinate in refrigerator overnight or for at least 8 hours. When ready to cook, pour off marinade and reserve. Bake chicken in a 350 degree oven for 1 hour. Baste with marinade while cooking. When done, sprinkle with paprika and serve with rice, pineapple rings, or mandarin oranges for a festive presentation. Or munch cold on a picnic.

Spotlight on Romance

★★

GARLIC SHRIMP

1/2 lb. **Butter**, melted
2 tbsp. **Olive Oil**
4 cloves **Garlic**, pressed
2 tbsp. fresh **Lime Juice**
1/4 cup minced fresh **Cilantro**
2 lbs. large or 3 lb. medium **Shrimp**, cooked, deveined, shelled

In small saucepan, blend butter, oil, garlic, lime juice and cilantro. Arrange shrimp on plates, pour small amount of butter sauce in individual bowls for dipping shrimp.

6 Servings

Bread, Wine & Thou

✦✦

A lovely little baguette and some soft cheese shared with your sweetie may be all you could wish for, but if you are thinking to zest up your meal with a little bit of the grape, this section can help guide the way.

Many of us have carried around the idea that only certain wines can be served with particular foods. What we have come to learn, however, is that while some flavors enhance each other, the ultimate decision on which bottle to slip from the rack is up to you. You know which wines you enjoy most, so regardless of what any wine connoisseurs may say, they will not be the ones sitting down to dine with you. Having cleared that up, we can now go on to say that, while wine rules may be a thing of the past, there are some guidelines that can help in giving those taste buds the ultimate treat: *

*W*ine Pairings

Fuller-bodied wines are likely to overpower lighter, more delicate dishes and lighter-bodied wines will get lost if paired with heavier foods. It has been suggested that if you drink a lighter style wine with roast beef, you might just as well drink water for the loss in taste you will encounter.

In a similar vein, the sauces you serve with your meal can affect your culinary experience. Lighter, creamier, more delicate sauces are better enhanced by lighter wines than heavier, tomato-based, spicy sauces or grilled meats.

Wine by itself offers one flavor experience. Mixed with food, it acts like a spice and offers quite another. Here are several possible reactions that can come from different types of foods:

Bread, Wine & Thou

****

- High Acid Foods go well with wines that are higher in acidic content. Examples of this: salads topped with vinaigrette dressing or fish served with a slice of lemon are provided a nice contrast by serving them with Sauvignon Blanc, Pinot Noir, Pinot Grigio or White Zinfandel.

- Sweet Foods can make your wine seem dryer than it really is. So if your meal includes sweeter dishes such as Japanese teriyaki, Italian tomato-based sauce or a honey-mustard type of glaze, try an off-dry, slightly sweet wine such as Riesling, Chenin Blanc or a White Zinfandel to balance the flavor.

- Bitter and Astringent Foods can heighten the bitterness in a wine. A salad of bitter greens, Greek kalamata olives, and charbroiled meats are best complimented with a full-flavored, fruity wine such as Chardonnay, Merlot or Cabernet Sauvignon. The fat in meats like grilled steak, pork or lamb chops will settle down the bitterness in wine when combined with tannic wines like red Zinfandels and Shiraz or Syrah.

Burgers and Wine

The burger has become one of America's most popular grilled foods and now it comes topped with a great variety of tasty additions. Once again, while only suggestions, these wine pairings may be just the thing to transform the ordinary grilled hamburger into a culinary feast. See what happens to your tongue when you combine these burger toppings and wines:

- Chili cheeseburger and Zinfandel
- Black pepper, gorgonzola cheese and hot mustard with Cabernet Sauvignon
- Pickle relish and yellow mustard with White Zinfandel
- Lettuce, tomato, raw red onion, ketchup and mayo with an Australian Shiraz or a California Syrah

Bread, Wine & Thou

★★★

- Grilled white onions and sautéed mushrooms and Swiss cheese with an Italian Chianti or a California Sangiovese
- Grilled pineapple with Chardonnay for the white wine lover or Beaujolais for those who prefer red
- Avocado, cucumber and sprouts with Sauvignon Blanc for lovers of the white and Merlot for those who lean more toward the red

Snacks and Wine

Yes, even simple snacks can be enhanced by a wine that reacts favorably with their essence! When you slip that bag of pretzels or chips into your picnic basket, remember to check out this list:

- Veggies and dip with a smooth and fruity Merlot or a crisp, dry Sauvignon Blanc
- Salsa and Nachos with Chardonnay or a spicy red wine like Zinfandel or Syrah
- Chips with a light crisp Pinot Gris or Italian Pinot Grigio to balance the oil and salt. Onion-flavored chips or chips served with sour cream dip and Merlot. Barbeque-flavored chips and Zinfandel
- Pretzels and mustard dip with a fruity White Zinfandel
- Mixed nuts or trail mix that has dried fruit with a soft, fruity wine like Beaujolais, Chianti or Sangiovese
- Pizza with Chardonnay or Pinot Grigio. Red wines such as Chianti, Syrah or Shiraz, and Zinfandel are also great with pizza
- Chinese egg rolls with Reisling or White Zinfandel to balance the spice

*Information gathered from www.wineanswers.com Felicia M. Sherbert, author of The Unofficial Guide to Selecting Wines.

★★

Salads

★★

Apple-Grape Celery Salad

Chilled Artichoke Salad

Grapefruit and Avocado Salad

Marcia's Sweet-Sour Slaw

Black Bean Salad

Carrot Salad

Aunt Betty's Cole Slaw

Potato Salad

Green Pepper Cole Slaw

Eastern-Style Cole Slaw

Fresh Corn Salad

Home-Style Cole Slaw

Cucumber-Onion Salad

Grandma Lucille's Cole Slaw

Fiesta Salad

Chunky Potato Salad

Hot Potato Salad

Potato Salad A La Pacific

Salads

★★

APPLE-GRAPE AND CELERY SALAD

4 large **Red Delicious Apples**
3 ribs **Celery**, chopped
1/3 cup halved **Seedless Grapes**
1/4 cup chopped **Walnuts**
3 tbsp. **Mayonnaise**
1 tsp. **Lemon Juice**
1/2 tsp. grated **Lemon Peel**
Pinch **Sugar**
Pinch **Salt**
Lettuce Leaves
Grapes for garnish

Core and cube apples; do not peel. In large bowl combine apples, celery, grapes and nuts. In small bowl mix mayonnaise, lemon juice and peel, sugar and salt. Fold.

Salads

★★

CHILLED ARTICHOKE SALAD

1 box **Rice-a-Roni®** chicken flavor
2 **Green Onions**, sliced...tops too
1/2 **Green Bell Pepper**, chopped
2 jars (6oz) **Marinated Artichoke Hearts**, chopped
1/4 tsp. **Curry Powder**
1/2 cup **Mayonnaise**

Cook rice as directed on box, with exception, do not brown in butter. Allow to stand until cool. Add chopped onions and green pepper. Drain artichoke hearts, reserving liquid. Add curry to mayonnaise, then mayonnaise to artichoke liquid and mix well. Combine with rice. Fold in artichoke hearts; chill. Delicious substitute for potato salad!

8 Servings

Salads

★★

GRAPEFRUIT AND AVOCADO SALAD

2 **Ruby Red Grapefruits**
2 **Avocados**, peeled and sliced
1 small **Purple Onion**, sliced
4 cups **Salad Greens**, torn into pieces

Peel, seed and section grapefruit. Combine with avocado slices, onion and salad greens. Toss gently with the following dressing. Refrigerate for 30 minutes before serving.

Dressing:
1/2 cup **Sugar**
1/2 tsp. **Dry Mustard**
3/4 tsp. **Salt**
1/4 cup **Vinegar**
3/4 cup **Vegetable Oil**
1 1/2 tbsp. **Poppy Seeds**

Beat all ingredients together until thoroughly mixed. Keep refrigerated.

Salads

★★★

BLACK BEAN SALAD

1 can (15oz) **Fat Free Black Beans**, drained and rinsed
1 can (14oz) **Diced Green Chiles**, drained
4 **Green Onions**, cut into 1/2 inch pieces
2 **Tomatoes**, chopped
1/4 tsp. **Garlic Salt**
Pepper, to taste
1 tbsp. **Lemon Juice**
2 tbsp. **Salsa**
1/2 head **Lettuce**, shredded

Combine all ingredients in a large bowl and toss well. Refrigerate for at least an hour or until thoroughly chilled.

4 Servings.

Salads

★★

Carrot Salad

1/2 lb. **Carrots**, grated, about 2 cups
1 tbsp. fresh **Lemon Juice**
1/8 tsp. **Salt**
1/4 cup miniature **Marshmallows**
1 can (81/2oz) **Pineapple Tidbits**
1 tbsp. **Honey**
1/4 tsp. **Nutmeg**
1/2 cup plain **Yogurt** or dairy **Sour Cream**

Combine grated carrots, lemon juice and salt. Add marshmallows and fruit. Blend honey and nutmeg with yogurt. Toss lightly with carrot mixture. Chill well. (Add 1/4 cup shredded coconut to carrot mixture before adding dressing, if desired.

Salads

★★★

AUNT BETTY'S COLE SLAW

1 package (16oz.) shredded **Cabbage**, chopped
1/2 cup shredded **Carrots**
1/2 cup **Heavy** or **Whipping Cream**
1/3 cup **Sugar**
2 1/2 tbsp. **Cider Vinegar**
1/2 tsp. **Salt**
Parsley Sprigs for garnish

In large bowl combine cabbage and carrots. In small bowl combine cream, sugar, vinegar and salt: stir until sugar dissolves. Pour over cabbage and toss until well coated. Cover and refrigerate until serving time.

Cole Slaw Tips
Start with deli or homemade cole slaw and: Stir in chopped mandarin oranges, chopped peanuts and sliced green onions. Add finely chopped red onion and a dash of sesame oil.

Salads

★★

GREEN PEPPER COLE SLAW

1 pound **Deli Cole Slaw**
1/3 cup chopped **Green Bell Pepper**
3 tbsp. minced **Onion**
1/2 cup **Raisins**
1/2 cup grated **Carrots**

In large bowl, toss together ingredients. Refrigerate until serving time.

MARCIA'S SWEET-SOUR SLAW

1 medium **Cabbage**, finely grated or chopped
1 medium **Onion**, sliced in fine circles
2 peeled **Carrots**, sliced in thin circles
2 **Green Bell Peppers**, sliced in thin circle
Salt and **Pepper**, to taste
1 cup **Vinegar**
1 cup **Sugar**
1 cup **Salad Oil**

Be sure that the onions, carrots and peppers are sliced very thin. Mix the vegetables, season with salt and pepper. Then add vinegar, sugar and salad oil to vegetables, mixing thoroughly.

10 Servings

$\mathcal{S}$alads

★★

HOME-STYLE COLE SLAW

2 tbsp. **Vinegar**
1 cup **Mayonnaise**
1 tsp. **Salt**
1/2 tsp. **Sugar**
1/2 tsp. ground **Black Pepper**
1/2 tsp. grated **Onion**
1 medium **Cabbage,** about 10 cups, shredded
2 **Carrots**, shredded
1/4 **Green Bell Pepper,** shredded

Combine vinegar with mayonnaise and stir until well blended. Add salt, sugar, pepper and onion and mix thoroughly. Chill until serving. Combine shredded cabbage, carrots and green pepper and toss with mayonnaise mixture until thoroughly coated.

8 Servings.

Salads

★★★

GRANDMA LUCILLE'S COLE SLAW

1 cup mild flavored **Honey**
1 cup **Wine Vinegar**
1/2 cup finely chopped **Onion**
1 tsp. **Salt**
1 tsp. **Celery Seed**
1 large **Cabbage**, finely chopped, 4 cups
1 cup diced **Green Pepper**
1 cup diced **Celery**

In a small saucepan, combine honey with vinegar, onion, salt, and celery seed. Bring to a boil, reduce heat and simmer five minutes. Cool. Pour the cooled dressing over prepared vegetables and toss lightly. Cover and chill several hours or overnight to blend flavors.

Salads

★★

EASTERN-STYLE SLAW

6 medium **Cabbage**, finely shredded
1 1/2 cups sliced **Green Onion**
1 1/2 quarts **Mayonnaise** or **Salad Dressing**
3/4 cup **Sugar**
3/4 cup **Vinegar**
2 to 4 tbsp. **Celery Seed**
2 tbsp. **Salt**, to taste

Combine cabbage and onion in a large bowl. In a smaller bowl, blend mayonnaise, sugar, vinegar, celery seed and salt. Mix well and drizzle mayonnaise mixture over cabbage mix. Toss lightly to coat well. Refrigerate until serving.

50 Servings.

Salads

★★

FRESH CORN SALAD

5 medium ears **Corn**
1 1/2 cups chopped **Celery**
1/2 cup chopped **Green Pepper**
3 **Eggs**, hard-cooked and chopped
2 tbsp. diced **Pimiento**
1/2 cup **Mayonnaise**
1 tsp. grated **Onion**
2 tsp. fresh **Lemon Juice**
1 tsp. **Sugar**
1 1/2 tsp. **Salt**, optional
1/8 tsp. **Pepper**

Boil corn, cool and cut from cob. Mix with celery, green pepper, eggs and pimento. Combine remaining ingredients. Stir into corn mixture. Chill.

6 Servings.

Salads

★★★

CUCUMBER-ONION SALAD

2 medium **Cucumbers**, peeled, seeded and sliced
2 **Green Onions**, sliced
1/2 tsp. **Salt**
1 tsp. **Sugar**
1 tbsp. **White Vinegar**
Dash **Red Pepper Sauce**

In medium bowl, toss cucumbers with green onion, salt, sugar, vinegar and red pepper sauce; toss well. Set aside for 10 minutes. Toss lightly before serving.

GREEN AND BLACK OLIVE SALAD

1 1/2 cups chopped
    Pimiento-stuffed Olives
1/2 cup chopped pitted **Ripe Olives**
1 large **Red** or **Green Bell Pepper**, chopped
1/3 cup chopped fresh **Parsley**
2 tbsp. drained **Capers**
2 tbsp. minced **Garlic**
1/2 tsp. **Oregano**
3/4 cup **Olive Oil**
1 tsp. **Red Wine Vinegar**

In medium bowl combine all ingredients. Cover and set aside at room temperature until serving time.

Salads

★★★

FIESTA SALAD

8 **Green Chiles**, roasted, peeled, seeded and chopped
2 **Tomatoes**, sliced
1 small **Red Onion**, coarsely chopped
1 **Cucumber**, peeled and sliced
1 each **Green, Red & Yellow Bell Pepper**, chopped
1/4 cup chopped, fresh **Cilantro**
3 tbsp. **Salsa**
2 tbsp. **Lemon Juice**
1/2 tsp. **Garlic Salt**
1/4 tsp. **Pepper**
1/4 tsp. **Ground Cumin**

Combine all ingredients and chill for at least one hour. Serve with baked tortilla chips or on a bed of lettuce.

6 Servings.

Salads

★★★

POTATO SALAD

3 lbs. **Potatoes**
2 cups diced **Celery**
1/4 cup finely chopped **Onion**
1/4 cup finely chopped fresh **Parsley**
1 cup **Mayonnaise**
2 tsp. **Vinegar**
1 tsp. **Salt**
1/4 tsp. **Ground Black Pepper**
Tomatoes, for garnish

Cook potatoes in boiling water until tender. Peel and Chill. Thinly slice chilled potatoes into mixing bowl. Add celery, onion, parsley, mayonnaise, vinegar, salt and pepper. Toss lightly until well mixed. Garnish with tomato slices.

8 Servings.

Potato Salad Tips
Dress up 1 pound Deli Potato Salad by adding:

1/4 cup chopped **Pimiento-Stuffed Green Olives**
2 Tbsp grated **Onion**
1/2 cup chopped, fresh **Tomato**
1/2 cup cubed **Ham**
1/4 cup chopped **Green Bell Pepper**

$\mathcal{S}$alads

★★

CHUNKY POTATO SALAD

4 **Potatoes**
1/2 cup chopped **Celery**
1/3 cup chopped **Onion**
3/4 cup **Mayonnaise**
1/4 cup **Milk**
1 tsp. **Salt**
1/4 tsp. **Ground Black Pepper**
1 tbsp. chopped fresh **Parsley**

Peel potatoes and cut into halves. Put halves into pan and add an inch of water. Bring water to a boil, cover potatoes, lower heat and simmer 20 minutes (until tender). Drain off cooking liquid when potatoes are done.

While potatoes are simmering, combine remaining ingredients into a salad bowl. Cut warm potatoes into chunks and add to salad bowl. Chill thoroughly before serving.

4 to 6 Servings.

Salads

★★

HOT POTATO SALAD

4 lbs. small **White Potatoes**
1 cup diced **Bacon**
1/2 cup minced **Onion**
1 1/2 tbsp. **Cornstarch**
1/4 cup **Sugar**
4 tsp. **Salt**
1/4 tsp. **Pepper**
3/4 cup **Vinegar**
1 1/2 cups **Water**
1/4 cup snipped fresh **Parsley**
1 cup diced **Celery**

Cook potatoes in jackets in boiling, salted water till fork-tender.

Peel and slice into 1/4 inch slices. In a skillet, fry bacon until crisp. Add minced onion and sauté until just tender, not brown. In a bowl, mix cornstarch, sugar, salt and pepper. Stir in vinegar and water and mix until smooth. Add to bacon and onion, stirring over low heat until slightly thickened. Pour this hot dressing over potatoes, parsley and celery which have been combined into a bowl. Toss and serve hot.

8 Servings.

Salads

★★

POTATO SALAD A LA PACIFIC

3 large **Potatoes**
1/3 cup dry **White Wine**
3 tbsp. **Salad Oil**
1 1/2 tsp. **Lemon Juice**
2 tbsp. minced **Onion**
1/2 medium **Cucumber**, diced
2 tbsp. chopped **Green Bell Pepper**
1/4 cup melted **Butter**
1 tsp. **Salt**
Pepper to taste

Boil potatoes in their jackets until tender. Peel and dice or slice.

Combine remaining ingredients; pour over potatoes and toss thoroughly.

Chill for several hours before serving, tossing occasionally so all pieces are well marinated. Serve in lettuce cups, garnished with tomato wedges.

4 Servings.

Sandwiches & Wraps

★★★

Chicken Lettuce Wraps

Chicken Salad with toasted Almonds Sandwich

Classic Heros

Dungeness Crab Sandwich

Grilled Mediterranean Veggie Sandwich

Real N'awlins Muffuletta

Quick Muffuletta

Smoked Turkey Wraps

Stuffed Blue-Cheese Burger

Taco Dogs

Mexican Burgers

Mighty Bacon Cheeseburgers

Too Juicy Burgers

BBQ Turkey Burgers

Spicy Homemade Burger

Homemade Veggie Burger

Sandwiches & Wraps

★★

CHICKEN LETTUCE WRAPS

2 tbsp. **Canola Oil**
1 tbsp. minced fresh **Ginger Root**
1 1/4 lbs. skinless, boneless **Chicken Breast halves**,
       cut into bite-sized pieces
2 tbsp. **Rice Vinegar**
2 tbsp. **Teriyaki Sauce**
1 tbsp. **Honey**
1 lb. dark **Sweet Cherries**, pitted and halved
1 1/2 cups shredded **Carrots**
1/2 cup chopped **Green Onion**
1/3 cup toasted and sliced **Almonds**
12 leaves of **Lettuce**

Heat 1 tablespoon oil in a large skillet over medium-high heat. Add ginger and chicken and sauté until cooked through, about 7 to 10 minutes. Set aside. In a large bowl, whisk together remaining 1 tablespoon oil, vinegar, teriyaki sauce and honey.

Add chicken mixture, cherries, carrot, green onion and almonds; toss together. To Serve: Spoon 1/12 of the chicken/cherry mixture onto the center of each lettuce leaf; roll up leaf around filling and serve.

Sandwiches & Wraps

★★

CHICKEN SALAD WITH
TOASTED ALMONDS SANDWICH

4 cups cubed, cooked **Chicken**
2 Tbsp fresh **Lemon Juice**
1 cup low-fat creamy **Salad Dressing** (e.g. Miracle Whip®)
1/2 tsp. **Salt**
1 cup **Pineapple Tidbits** in juice, drained
1 cup halved **Green Grapes**
1/2 cup blanched slivered **Almonds**, toasted
1/2 cup chopped canned **Water Chestnuts**
1 head green **Leaf Lettuce**, rinsed
16 slices **Sara Lee® Soft & Smooth Whole Grain White Bread**

In a large bowl, toss the chicken with the lemon juice. Cover and chill for 2 hours.

Mix the salad dressing, salt, pineapple, grapes, almonds and water chestnuts into the chicken until well blended. Chill until serving. Serve on tasted bread with lettuce leaves.

Sandwiches & Wraps

★★★

CLASSIC HEROES

1/4 lb thinly sliced **Salami**
1/2 lb sliced **Provolone Cheese**
1/2 lb sliced **Ham**
4 6-8" **Hero Rolls**, split
2 medium **Tomatoes**, sliced
1 small **Onion**, thinly sliced
2 cups shredded **Iceberg Lettuce**
Bottled **Italian Dressing**

Layer salami, cheese and ham on bottom halves of rolls; top with tomato slices, onion slices and lettuce. Sprinkle dressing over lettuce. Replace tops of rolls.

Sandwich Tips

Deli Heroes: Slice French bread horizontally and pile on Swiss cheese, bologna, olive loaf, tomato and lettuce; sprinkle with salad dressing.

Juniors: Spread peanut butter on cracked wheat bread slices; add apple rings, American cheese and lettuce; top with second bread slices.

Whole Wheat Roll-Ups: Spread whole wheat bread slices with guacamole, then sprinkle with bean sprouts or alfalfa sprouts; roll up jelly-roll fashion. Secure with toothpicks.

Sandwiches & Wraps

****

DUNGENESS CRAB SANDWICH

2 slices **Sour Dough** or **French Bread**
2 slices **Jarlsberg Cheese** (may substitute Swiss)
2 ounces **Thousand Island Dressing**
4 ounces **Crab Meat** (Snow, Dungeness, Rock or Lump Crab)
2 tbsp. softened **Butter**
1 ripe **Avocado**, halved and peeled

Place the crab and avocado in a pan under the broiler to warm. Spread butter on the outside of both slices of bread for each sandwich, and the Thousand Island Dressing on the other side. Place the bread, butter side down, in a medium-hot skillet. Layer on the slices of cheese, warm crab and avocado. Add the remaining slice of bread and cook until golden brown.

Sandwiches & Wraps

★★★

GRILLED MEDITERRANEAN VEGGIE SANDWICH

1 **Eggplant**, sliced into strips
2 **Red Bell Peppers**
2 tbsp. **Olive Oil**, divided
2 **Portobello Mushrooms**, sliced
3 cloves **Garlic**, crushed
4 tbsp. **Mayonnaise**
1 (1 lb) loaf **Focaccia Bread**

Preheat oven to 400 degrees.

Brush eggplant and red bell peppers with 1 tablespoon olive oil; use more if necessary, depending on sizes of vegetables. Place on a baking sheet and roast in preheated oven. Roast eggplant until tender, about 25 minutes; roast peppers until blackened.  Remove from oven and set aside to cool. Meanwhile, heat 1 tablespoon olive oil and sauté mushrooms until tender. Stir crushed garlic into mayonnaise. Slice focaccia in half lengthwise. Spread mayonnaise mixture on one or both halves. Peel cooled peppers, core and slice. Arrange eggplant, peppers and mushrooms on focaccia. Wrap sandwich in plastic wrap; place a cutting board on top of it and weight it down with some canned foods. Allow sandwich to sit for 2 hours before slicing and serving.

Sandwiches & Wraps

★★

REAL N'AWLINS MUFFULETTA

1 cup crushed **Pimiento-stuffed Green Olives**
1/2 cup crushed drained **Kalamata Olives**
2 cloves **Garlic**, minced
1/4 cup roughly chopped pickled **Cauliflower Florets**
2 tbsp. drained **Capers**
1 tbsp. chopped **Celery**
1 tbsp. chopped **Carrot**
1/2 cup drained **Pepperoncini**
1/4 cup marinated **Cocktail Onions**
1/2 tsp. **Celery Seed**
1 tsp. dried **Oregano**
1 tsp. dried **Basil**
3/4 tsp. **Ground Black Pepper**
1/4 cup **Red Wine Vinegar**
1/2 cup **Olive Oil**
1/4 cup **Canola Oil**
2 (1 lb) loaves **Italian Bread**
8 oz. thinly sliced **Genoa Salami**
8 oz. thinly sliced cooked **Ham**
8 oz. sliced **Mortadella**
8 oz. sliced **Mozzarella Cheese**
8 oz. sliced **Provolone Cheese**

To Make Olive Salad: In a medium bowl, combine the green olives, kalamata olives, garlic, cauliflower, capers, celery, carrot, pepperoncini, cocktail onions, celery seed, oregano, basil, black pepper, vinegar, olive oil and canola oil. Mix together and transfer mixture into a glass jar (or other nonreactive container). If needed, pour in more oil to cover. Cover jar or container and refrigerate at least overnight.

★★

To Make Sandwiches: Cut loaves of bread in half horizontally; hollow out some of the excess bread to make room for filling. Spread each piece of bread with equal amounts of olive salad, including oil. Layer "bottom half" of each loaf with 1/2 of the salami, ham, mortadella, mozzarella and Provolone. Replace "top half" on each loaf and cut sandwich into quarters. Serve immediately, or wrap tightly and refrigerate for a few hours; this will allow for the flavors to mingle and the olive salad to soak into the bread.

QUICK MUFFULETTA

1 round (8 in.) loaf **Italian Bread**
1 recipe **Green** and **Black Olive Salad**
1/4 lb thinly sliced **Salami**
1/4 lb sliced **Provolone Cheese**
1/4 lb sliced **Ham**
1/2 lb sliced **Mozzarella Cheese**

With serrated knife, slice about 1/2 inch from top of Italian bread loaf. Cut and scoop out interior, leaving a 1/2 inch shell. Drain Olive Salad, reserving dressing. Brush interior of shell with reserved dressing; then layer with 1 1/2 cups Olive Salad, salami, provolone, ham, mozzarella and remaining salad. Replace top of loaf.

Sandwiches & Wraps

****

Smoked Turkey Wraps

10 **Whole Wheat Flour Tortillas**
10 slices **Smoked Turkey,**
    cut into thin strips
1 **Avocado**, peeled, pitted and sliced
1/2 cup **Sour Cream**, for topping
1/2 cup **Cheddar Cheese**

Heat flour tortillas in a large skillet over medium heat, until slightly browned. In each tortilla arrange turkey strips topped with avocado, sour cream and cheese. Fold up and serve with salsa.

Sandwiches & Wraps

STUFFED BLUE-CHEESE BURGER

8 **Sirloin Burgers**, pre-made, thawed from your grocer or butcher
1 cup crumbled **Blue Cheese**
4 **Multi-grain Sandwich Rolls**

Evenly distribute 1 cup of crumbled blue cheese on 4 burgers. Place a second burger on top of each and gently press together to keep blue cheese from falling out. Grill at medium heat until the meat is thoroughly cooked and the blue cheese is melted. Serve on a multi-grain roll.

Great additions to this burger include sautéed mushrooms or red onions.

Sandwiches & Wraps

★★

TACO DOGS

8 **Frankfurters**, sliced in half lengthwise
1 jar (8oz.) mild **Taco Sauce**
4 **Taco Shells**, heated
1 cup shredded **Cheddar Cheese**
1 cup shredded **Lettuce**
1 cup **Sour Cream**

In medium saucepan combine hot dogs and taco sauce; bring to a boil. Spoon into heated taco shells and top with cheese, lettuce and sour cream.

MEXICAN BURGERS

1 cup chopped **Green Onions**
1 cup bottled **Salsa**
1/4 tsp. **Cumin**
Dash **Salt**
1 lb. **Ground Beef**
Flour Tortillas, warmed
1 can (15 oz.) **Refried Beans**
Shredded Lettuce

Prepare grill or preheat broiler. In medium bowl combine 2 tablespoons green onions, 2 tablespoons salsa, cumin and salt with ground beef. Mix lightly and shape into 4 oval patties. Grill or broil 4 to 6 inches from heat, 3 minutes on each side. Place burgers in the center of warm tortillas. Top with refried beans, green onions, lettuce and salsa. Fold one side of tortilla up and the two adjacent sides inward. Fold fourth side over to enclose burger.

4-6 Servings

Sandwiches & Wraps

★★★

MIGHTY BACON CHEESEBURGERS

2 lbs. lean **Hamburger**
8 slices pre-cooked **Bacon**
1 cup shredded **Cheese**
Salt and **Pepper** to taste

Preheat gas grill for 10 minutes with burners on high.

Make 8 burgers that are thin and wide. Place a slice of bacon in the center of each burger and sprinkle with cheese. Add salt and pepper. Fold edges in to seal the center.

Turn burners to medium. Using lean hamburger will reduce the fat drippings, thus causing less flaming that can burn meat.

Place burgers on grill and close lid. Cook 3 minutes per side for rare, 5 minutes for medium and 7 minutes for well done. Remember, they will take a little longer than usual because they are thicker.

Don't forget to toast the buns on the grill!

8 Servings

TOO JUICY BURGERS
By Permission; Lea & Perrins, Inc.

1 lb. **Ground Beef**
2 tbsp. chopped **Onion**
2 tbsp. **Lea & Perrins® Steak Sauce**

In a medium bowl, combine beef, onion and two tablespoons of the Lea & Perrins® Steak Sauce. Shape into four 3 1/2 inch patties. Cook on a grill over hot coals. Makes 4 burgers.

Sandwiches & Wraps

★★★

BBQ Turkey Burgers

1 1/2 lbs. **Ground Turkey**
Salt and **Pepper** to taste
Barbecue Sauce of choice

Preheat gas grill for 10 minutes with
burners on high

Mix salt, pepper and 1 cup of your
favorite barbecue sauce into the
meat. Shape into 4 burgers. Turn burners to medium. Place burgers on grill.
Baste tops of burgers with sauce. Close lid and cook 6 minutes for medium
and 8 minutes for well done. Be sure to baste after flipping. 4 Servings

Don't forget to toast the buns on the grill!

Spicy Homemade Burger

1 lb. **Ground Beef**
1 large **Onion**, diced
1/8 cup **Breadcrumbs**
1 medium fresh **Jalapeno Pepper**, diced
1 tbsp. chopped fresh **Cilantro**
1 tsp. **Paprika**

Combine all ingredients in mixing bowl. Cover and chill for 30 minutes.
Divide into 4 portions, form into patties and grill to desired doneness

★★

HOMEMADE VEGGIE BURGER

4 oz. **Firm Tofu**, crumbled
1 **Egg**
1 small **Onion**, minced
1 tbsp. **Breadcrumbs**
1 stalk **Celery**, minced
1 tsp. **Vegetable Bouillon Powder**
1 tsp. **Soy or Worcestershire Sauce**
Salt and **Pepper** to taste

Mix all ingredients, shape into burgers and refrigerate for 15 minutes. Place on sheet of foil and grill for 5 minutes, turning after 2 minutes, or pan-fry in shallow oil.

Note: For cheesy burger, Before chilling the burger, push a small cube of your favorite cheese into the center. Brie or sharp cheddar is recommended. During the grilling stage, the cheese will melt into a tasty pocket.

★★★

Picnic Favorites

★★★

Flank Steaks with Rum

Marinated London Broil

Short Ribs Hawaiian Style

Marinated BBQ Chuck Steak

Chicken Vegetable Kabobs

Barbecued Chicken with Sherry

Tropical Chicken

Fried Picnic-Style Chicken

Southwest Ham

Spicy Sirloin

Barbecue Brisket

Sweetheart Breakfast Casserole

Oriental Chicken

Rummed Ham and Beans

Picnic Favorites

★★

FLANK STEAKS WITH RUM

4 8 oz. **Flank Steaks**

Marinade:
2 cups **Rum**
2 cups **Water**
2 tbsp. **Black Molasses**
2 tbsp. **Brown Sugar**
2 tbsp. **Honey**

Mix marinade ingredients in a bowl and pour over steaks. Marinate in refrigerator for one hour.

Preheat gas grill for 10 minutes with burners on high.

Turn burners to medium and place steaks on grill, reserving marinade. Close grill lid. Cook 3 minutes per side for rare, 5 minutes for medium and 8 minutes for well done. Baste with remaining marinade when flipping.

4 Servings

Picnic Favorites

****

MARINATED LONDON BROIL

1 1/2 lbs. **Flank Steak**

Marinade:
1/2 cup **Steak Sauce**
2 tsp. **Worcestershire Sauce**
4 tsp. **Lemon Juice**
1/4 tsp. **Salt**

Prick steak several times on both sides with fork tines and place in a shallow glass pan. Combine balance of ingredients and pour over steak. Marinate for one hour. Grill 10 to 15 minutes, turning and brushing often with marinade.

4-6 Servings

Picnic Favorites

★★

SHORT RIBS HAWAIIAN STYLE

4 to 5 lbs. lean **Beef Short Ribs**, cut in 2 inch lengths

Marinade:
1 tbsp. **Butter**
1 tbsp. **Sesame Seeds**
1 cup **Soy Sauce**
3/4 cup **Red Wine**
1/2 cup **Red Wine Vinegar**
4 **Green Onions**, diced
1 medium **Onion**, diced
2 large cloves **Garlic**, minced
1 1/2 tbsp. **Brown Sugar**
1 tbsp. **Vegetable Oil**
2 tsp. minced fresh **Ginger Root**

Melt butter in a large saucepan and add sesame seeds. Cook until seeds are light brown. Add balance of ingredients and simmer until well-blended. Place ribs in a shallow glass dish. Pour marinade over ribs, cover and marinate in refrigerator for at least 8 hours. Grill over low flame, turning and brushing with sauce occasionally.

Picnic Favorites

MARINATED BBQ CHUCK STEAK
Gloria Huggins—Madison, Florida

2-3 lbs. **Chuck Steak**

Marinade:
1/3 cup **Olive Oil**
2 tsp. **Ground Ginger**
2 tbsp. minced **Onion**
1 tbsp. **Chili Powder**
1 tsp. **Salt**
1/4 cup **Lemon Juice**

Combine all ingredients for marinade. Place steak in shallow glass dish. Pour marinade over steak, cover and marinate in refrigerator for several hours, or overnight. Place steak on grill, cooking 8 to 10 minutes on each side, or until desired degree of doneness.

4-6 Servings

Picnic Favorites

★★

CHICKEN VEGETABLE KABOBS

4 de-boned **Chicken Breasts**
24 **Cherry Tomatoes**
6 small **Onions**
3 **Green Bell Peppers**
3 **Lemons**

Preheat gas grill for 10 minutes with burners on high.

Slice chicken into 24 pieces. Cut onions into quarters. Cut green bell peppers and lemons into eighths.

Place chicken and vegetables on skewers (if using wooden skewers, soak in water for 20 minutes before using). Alternate in any pattern, but best to have peppers beside chicken.

Turn burners to medium and place skewers on grill. Close grill lid. Cook 5 minutes per side, or until chicken is done.

Remove from skewers and serve.

4 Servings

BARBECUED CHICKEN WITH SHERRY

4 **Chicken Breasts**
4 **Chicken Legs** or **Thighs**

Marinade:
1/2 cup **California Sherry**
2 tsp. **Cinnamon**
1/2 tsp. **Curry Powder**
1/3 cup **Honey**
2 tbsp. **Lemon Juice**
1 tsp. **Garlic Salt**

Combine all ingredients and marinate chicken pieces for several hours in refrigerator, turning occasionally. Grill until tender, basting with remaining marinade. Watch carefully, for the chicken will brown quickly. 8 Servings

Note: Chicken breasts cook faster than dark meat (legs, thighs).

Picnic Favorites

★★

TROPICAL CHICKEN

6 de-boned and skinned **Chicken Breast Halves**

Marinade:
1/3 cup **Pineapple Juice**
1 tbsp. **Vegetable Oil**
1 tsp. **Salt**
1 tsp. **Ground Ginger**
1/4 tsp. **Ground Tumeric**
1/2 tsp. **Ground Thyme**
1/4 tsp. **Crushed Hot Red Pepper Flakes**

Combine all marinade ingredients in a large glass dish and whisk until well blended. Rinse chicken with cold water and pat dry. Add chicken to marinade, place in refrigerator for 2 to 4 hours, turning several times. Grill, turning once and basting occasionally with remaining marinade, until chicken is white throughout and still juicy, about 8 minutes per side.

6 Servings

Picnic Favorites

✦✦✦

Fried Picnic-Style Chicken

3 lbs. **Chicken,** cut up
2 cups **Buttermilk**

Soak Chicken in buttermilk
overnight in refrigerator.

Next day, mix:
2 cups **Flour**
1 tsp. **Black Pepper**
1 tsp. **Paprika**
1 tsp. **Garlic Salt**
1 tsp. **Dried Parsley**

Lift chicken pieces one at a time out of buttermilk and roll in flour mixture.
Pat flour on, repeat until all pieces are covered. Fry in oil over medium heat
until chicken is done. Drain on paper towels.

Southwest Ham

2 slices (1 lb. each) 1/4 inch thick **Ham**
1/3 cup raspberry or other flavored **Mustard**
1/3 cup **Vegetable Oil**
1 can (15 oz.) **Tomatoes with Chilies**
1 can (12 oz.) **Mandarin Orange Slices**
1/3 cup **Tequila**

Coat ham slices with mustard and fry in oil. Slash edges to prevent curling.
When well-browned, remove from skillet, add remaining ingredients,
cover and simmer for 1 hour. Remove cover, increase heat and reduce any
remaining liquid. Serve with pan drippings.

6 Servings

Picnic Favorites

★★

SPICY SIRLOIN

2 lbs. **Sirloin Steak**
1/4 cup **Vegetable Oil**
1/2 tsp. **Chili Powder**
1 tsp. dried **Cilantro Flakes**
1/2 tsp. dried **Oregano**

In small bowl, combine oil, chili powder, cilantro and oregano. Pour over steak. Let stand one hour then grill to desired doneness.

4-5 Servings

BARBECUE BRISKET

4-5 lb. **Beef Brisket**
1 cup **Mayonnaise**
1 cup bottled **Chili Sauce**
2 tbsp. **Worcestershire Sauce**
3 tbsp. **Crushed Red Pepper**
Garlic Salt to taste

Place brisket in large baking pan. In medium bowl, combine all other ingredients, pour over meat, cover tightly with foil and bake in 300 degree oven for 5-6 hours.

6-8 Servings

Picnic Favorites

****

SWEETHEART BREAKFAST CASSEROLE
Denise Miller
Gourmet Country Style
Kensington Co-op Association

1 1/2 lbs. bulk **Sausage**, cooked and drained
8-9 slices **Bread**, crumbled
1/2 tsp. **Salt**
1 tsp. **Mustard**
1 tsp. **Worcestershire Sauce**
6 oz. **Swiss Cheese**, grated
6 oz. **Cheddar Cheese**, grated
6 oz. **Monterey Jack Cheese**, grated
6 **Eggs**, slightly beaten
3/4 cup + 2 tbsp. **Evaporated Milk**
1/1/2 cup **Milk**

Mix salt, mustard, worcestershire sauce and sausage. Pour over bread. Sprinkle cheeses on top.

Combine eggs, evaporated milk and milk. Pour over all. Refrigerate in 9x13 pan until baking.

Bake in 350 degree oven for 45 minutes or until eggs are set and top is well browned. Cool 5-10 minutes and serve.

Note: Must be prepared one day in advance and refrigerated overnight.

Ideal for a romantic breakfast.

Picnic Favorites

****

ORIENTAL CHICKEN

2 lbs. **Chicken Breasts**

Marinade:
6 tbsp. **Soy Sauce**
3 cloves **Garlic**, crushed
1/2 cup fresh **Lime Juice**
1/2 tsp. **Ground Ginger**
Rinse chicken, pat dry and place in glass baking pan. In small bowl, combine soy sauce, garlic, lime juice and ginger. Mix well, pour over chicken. Marinate several hours or overnight. Grill until done, brushing occasionally with extra marinade.

4 Servings

RUMMED HAM AND BEANS

2 cans (16 oz.) **Pork and Beans**
1 lb. cooked **Ham**, diced
1 small **Onion**, chopped
1 tsp. **Ground Cloves**
1 tsp. **Dry Mustard**
1/4 cup **Dark Rum**

Place beans in medium baking dish, top with diced ham. In small bowl, mix together onion, cloves and mustard. Sprinkle evenly over ham and beans. Bake in 325 degree oven for 1 hour. Remove from oven, pour rum over all and bake an additional 15 minutes.

4-6 Servings

★★★

Side Dishes

★★★

Hobo Beans

Bean-N-Bacon Bake

Deviled Eggs

Deviled Eggs without Mayonnaise

Tuna and Veggie Platter

Corn Custard

Red Potatoes

Perfect Petite Peas

Cilantro Salsa

Pita Chips

Easy Spaghetti Pasta

Side Dishes

★★

Hobo Beans

1 cup **Brown Sugar**
1 cup **Sugar**
1/2 cup **Barbecue Sauce**
1/2 cup **Ketchup**
1/4 cup **Mustard**
1/2 cup cooked and finely chopped **Bacon**
1/2 tbsp **Salt**
1 tbsp. **Worcestershire Sauce**
1/2 tbsp. **Tabasco® Sauce**
1/2 tbsp. **Louisiana Hot Sauce**
1/2 cup **Water**
1 can (64 oz) **Baked Beans**

Combine ingredients and simmer for 30 minutes.

Tip: If you would like to make authentic hobo beans, add a half pound Larry's Crossing® Chopped barbecue. As an alternative, add 1/2 pound browned ground beef.

Side Dishes

★★★

BEAN-N-BACON BAKE

2 cups (16 oz. can) **Baked Beans**
1/4 cup firmly packed **Brown Sugar**
1/2 cup **Catsup**
1 tsp. **Worcestershire Sauce**
1 tbsp. grated **Onions**
1 tsp. **Salt**
1 tsp. **Vinegar**
1 lb. **Bacon**

Combine all ingredients in a 6-cup baking dish. Cut bacon into slices and spread on top. Bake in 400 degree oven 40 minutes or until beans are bubbly and bacon is crisp.

Side Dishes

★★

DEVILED EGGS

6 **Eggs**, hard boiled
1/4 cup **Mayonnaise**
1/4 tsp. **Salt**
Pepper, to taste (lemon-pepper is perfect)
2 tsp. prepared **Mustard**
1 tbsp. minced **Onion**
1 tbsp. **Sweet Pickle Relish**

Optional: Celery, Crumbled Bacon, Olives, Pimento, you name it.

Halve hard boiled eggs and remove yolks. Mash yolks and combine with remaining ingredients. Refill egg whites with mounds of yolk mixture and trim with parsley and/or paprika. Eliminate a couple of whites for plumper eggs. If the eggs "wobble" cut a thin slice off the base.

TIP: to avoid cracking shells while cooking, have eggs at room temperature. Place in a pan of hot water for about 3 minutes. Place on stove burner and bring to a slow boil, cooking for a total of 5 minutes. It is important to run eggs immediately under cold water (about 5 minutes) for easy shell removal.

$\mathcal{S}$ide $\mathcal{D}$ishes

★★★

DEVILED EGGS WITHOUT MAYONNAISE

6 **Eggs**, hard boiled
3/4 cup **Chicken Stock**
2 tsp. unflavored **Powdered Gelatin**, softened in 3 tbsp. cold water
1 tsp. prepared **Mustard**
1 tsp chopped fresh **Parsley**
1/2 tsp. **Salt**
1/2 tsp. **Worcestershire sauce**

Cut the eggs in half crosswise, remove the yolks, and cut off the tips from the narrower ends of the egg whites to make straight-standing cups. The broader ends of the eggs usually do not require leveling. Press the yolks through a sieve.

Heat the chicken stock to the boiling point; add the softened gelatin and stir to dissolve it. Reheat the stock a bit if necessary. Add the mustard, parsley, salt and Worcestershire Sauce. Chill the mixture until it begins to jell. Beat the mixtures lightly, then add the egg yolks. The mixture should now be just right for pressing through a pastry tube. If not, refrigerate it until it is a bit firmer.

Using the pastry tube, fill the egg cups with the mixture.

Side Dishes

****

TUNA AND VEGGIE PLATTER

1/2 bunch **Broccoli**
3/4 cup **Mayonnaise**
1/4 cup **Plain Yogurt**
1 small clove **Garlic**, halved
1 tbsp. **Dijon Mustard**
1 cup canned **Red Kidney Beans**, drained and rinsed
1 can (14 oz) **Artichoke Hearts**, drained
1 package (10 oz) frozen **Asparagus Spears**, thawed
2 **Tomatoes** cut into wedges
1 can (13 oz) **Tuna**, drained

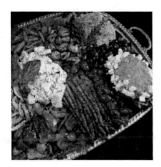

Cut off broccoli florets and plunge into salted boiling water; cook 4 minutes. (Save stems and remaining broccoli for another meal.) Drain and plunge into cold water to cool. Drain again. In small bowl combine mayonnaise, yogurt, garlic and mustard. Arrange broccoli, remaining vegetables and tuna on serving platter. Spoon half the mayonnaise-mustard dressing over top; serve remainder in small bowl.

Side Dishes

****

CORN CUSTARD

1 can (15 oz.) **Whole Kernel Corn**, drained
3 **Eggs**
1/4 tsp. **Nutmeg**
2 tbsp. **Sugar**
1/8 tsp. **Pepper**
1 cup **Milk**
1 cup **Cream**

This recipe uses canned corn but if fresh corn is available use 8 ears and add 2 tbsps. of extra sugar.

Place corn in large bowl. Beat eggs, add to corn along with remaining ingredients. Stir well. Pour into 8x8 buttered baking dish. Place dish into large dish, fill with water 1 inch deep. Bake in 350 degree oven for 1 hour or until knife inserted into center comes out clean.

6 Servings

RED POTATOES

2 lbs. **Red Potatoes**, cubed
2 tbsp**. Crushed Red Peppers**
1 tbsp. **Parsley Flakes**
1 tsp. **Salt**
4 tbsp. **Butter**

Cook cubed potatoes in water to cover in large saucepan until done. Drain potatoes thoroughly. Return to pan. Add remaining ingredients and toss gently to coat potatoes. Serve hot, or cold as a salad. Wonderful with beef.

6 Servings

Side Dishes

★★

PERFECT PETITE PEAS

3 packages frozen **Petite Peas**
1/2 cup chopped **Onions**
1 cup canned or fresh **Mushrooms**
2 tbsp. **Olive Oil**
8 oz. **Sour Cream**

Cook peas according to package directions. Drain and set aside. Sauté onions and mushrooms in oil until onions are limp and slightly browned. Stir in peas to heat. Remove from heat, stir in sour cream. Serve warm, or cold as a salad.

4 Servings

CILANTRO SALSA

4 medium **Tomatoes**, diced
1 small **Onion**, diced
1 **Bell Pepper**, any color, diced
1 can (4 oz.) diced **Green Chilies**, drained
1/2 tsp. dried **Oregano**
1/4 tsp. **Salt**
1/2 cup fresh **Cilantro**
1 tbsp. **Orange Juice**

Combine all ingredients in medium bowl. Serve chilled or at room temperature.

Makes about 2 cups.

Side Dishes

★★

PITA CHIPS

Flour Tortillas

Homemade pita chips couldn't be simpler. Just take each tortilla and slice it into 8 pieces, 'pizza' style. Put in 350 degree oven for 30 minutes or until they have dried out completely.

EASY SPAGHETTI PASTA

1/2 lb. **Spaghetti**, cooked, drained, cooled
12 **Cherry** or **Grape Tomatoes**, halved
1 bottle (16 oz.) **Zesty Italian Salad Dressing**
2 **Cucumbers**, diced
1 large **Red Bell Pepper**, diced
1 small **Onion**, diced

In a large bowl, mix all of the ingredients except the salad dressing. Add as much salad dressing as you like. Leave to chill for 8 hours or overnight. Serve cold.

★★★

Desserts

★★★

Brownies and Frosting

Brownies

Delicious Oatmeal Cookies

Fudgey Raspberry Brownies

Easy-Cheesy Lemon Bars

Lemon Crumb Squares

Apple Pie Cheddar Sundae

Oatmeal Cookies

S'more Brownies

Three Sherbet Cooler

Snickerdoodles

Super Peanut Butter Cookies

Desserts

****

BROWNIES AND FROSTING

2 cups **Sugar**
1 cup **Shortening**
4 **Eggs**
1 1/2 cups **Flour**
1/3 cup **Cocoa**
1/4 tsp. **Salt**
3 tsp. **Vanilla**
1/2 cup chopped **Walnuts**
6 oz. miniature **White Marshmallows**

Cream sugar, shortening and eggs. Add dry ingredients, vanilla and nuts. Spread in sprayed baking dish and bake at 350 degrees approximately 20 minutes, or until almost done. Spread marshmallows on baked base. Return to oven for about 10 minutes, or until marshmallows are lightly browned. Cool before frosting.

FROSTING

2 sticks (1 cup) melted **Margarine**
1/3 cup **Cocoa**
1 lb. box **Confectioners Sugar**
1/4 cup **Whole Milk**
1 tsp. **Vanilla**
1/2 cup chopped **Walnuts**

Melt margarine in large saucepan. Add all ingredients, except nutmeats, to melted margarine. Beat with electric mixer until smooth. Add walnuts and frost. Best to refrigerate an hour to set icing, but no need to refrigerate again. Great glorified brownie!

Desserts

★★

BROWNIES

1 cup **Butter**
4 oz. **Unsweetened Chocolate**
4 **Eggs**
2 cups **Sugar**
1 cup **Flour**
1 tsp. **Baking Powder**
1/4 tsp. **Salt**
2 tsp. **Vanilla**
1 cup chopped **Walnuts**

Preheat oven to 350 degrees. Melt butter and chocolate together in small saucepan. Using electric mixer, beat together eggs, sugar, flour, baking powder, salt and vanilla. Combine melted chocolate mixture with batter; beat well. Fold in chopped nuts and spread in sprayed 13x9x2 baking dish. Bake for 25 minutes or until toothpick inserted in center comes out clean. Serve plain, sprinkled with sifted powdered sugar, or cool and frost with half a batch of frosting above. Rich, moist brownies.

Desserts

★★★

DELICIOUS OATMEAL COOKIES

1 cup **Shortening**
1 cup **Granulated Sugar**
1 cup **Brown Sugar**
2 **Eggs**
1 tsp. **Vanilla**
1/2 tsp. **Baking Powder**
1 tsp. **Baking Soda**
1/2 tsp. **Salt**
2 cups **Flour**
2 cups quick **Oatmeal**
1 pkg. (6oz.) **Chocolate Chips**
1/2 cup each: **Walnuts and Raisins**

Preheat oven to 350 degrees. Cream shortening and sugar, add eggs and vanilla and beat well. Combine baking powder, baking soda, salt and flour; blend well into shortening mixture. Add oatmeal, chips, nuts and raisins. Bake 10 – 15 minutes on sprayed or waxed paper-lined baking sheet. (Trim paper edges to fit cookie sheet.)

Desserts

FUDGEY RASPBERRY BROWNIES

1 1/4 cup (2 1/2 sticks) **Butter**
2 cups **Sugar**
2 tsp. **Vanilla**
4 **Eggs**
1 1/2 cups **All Purpose Flour**
3/4 cup **Cocoa**
1 8oz. pkg. **Dark Chocolate filled w/Raspberry Crème Baking Pieces**
3/4 to 1 cup chopped **Pecans**

Heat oven to 350 degrees. Grease 13x9x2 baking pan. Melt butter in medium saucepan over low heat. Remove from heat; stir in sugar and vanilla. Add eggs, one at a time, beating just until blended. Combine flour, cocoa; gradually add to butter mixture, stirring just until blended. Do not over mix. Add nuts. Spread batter into prepared pan. Sprinkle with the premier baking pieces. Bake 35 minutes or until wooden pick inserted in center comes out clean. Sprinkle with powdered sugar. Cool completely in pan on wire rack. Cut into squares.

Desserts

★★★

Easy-Cheesy Lemon Bars

1 box **Lemon Cake Mix**
1/2 cup melted **Butter or Margarine**
1 **Egg**
1 pkg. (16 oz) **Butter Cream Lemon Frosting Mix**
8 oz. **Cream Cheese.** softened
2 **Eggs**

Preheat oven to 350 degrees. Combine cake mix, butter and egg; stir until moist. Pat into sprayed baking dish. Blend frosting mix into softened cream cheese. (Reserve 1/2 cup for frosting.) Add eggs to remaining mixture. Beat 3 to 5 minutes and spread evenly over base; bake 20  to 30 minutes. Allow to cool before frosting. Easy and so good!

Desserts

★★

LEMON CRUMB SQUARES

1 (14 oz.) can **Sweetened Condensed Milk**
1/2 cup **Lemon Juice**
1 tsp. grated **Lemon Rind**
2/3 cup **Butter**
1 cup firmly packed **Dark Brown Sugar**
1 1/2 cups **Flour**
1 tsp. **Baking Powder**
1/2 tsp. **Salt**
1 cup quick **Oatmeal**

Preheat oven to 350 degrees. In medium bowl, blend condensed milk, lemon juice and rind; set aside. In larger mixing bowl, cream butter with sugar. Add flour through oatmeal and mix until crumbly. Spread 1/2 crumbly mixture in sprayed baking dish, patting down with fingers. Spread condensed milk mixture over top, followed by remaining crumb mixture. Bake 25 minutes or until light brown around edges. Cool in pan at room temperature approximately 15 minutes. Cut into squares or bars. Chill in pan until firm. (Not necessary to store in refrigerator once chilled.)

Desserts

★★

APPLE PIE CHEDDAR SUNDAE

1 quart **Vanilla Ice Cream**
1 can (21oz.) **Apple Pie Filling**
Cheddar Cheese Crackers, crushed

Place 2 small scoops ice cream in each dish.
Spoon on apple pie filling and top with crushed
crackers.

Desserts

★★

OATMEAL COOKIES

1 cup **Butter**
1/2 cup **Granulated Sugar**
3/4 cup **Brown Sugar**
2 **Eggs**
1/3 cup **Buttermilk**
1 1/2 tsp. **Vanilla**
1 tsp. **Salt**
1/2 tsp. **Cinnamon**
1 tsp. **Baking Soda**
2 cups **Flour**
3 cups quick **Oatmeal**
1/2 cup each: **Coconut, Raisins, Dates, Walnuts**

Preheat oven to 375 degrees. Combine ingredients in order presented; mixing well after each addition. Drop by spoonful on sprayed or wax-lined baking sheet. Bake 10 to 12 minutes for moist, soft cookies. Do not over bake!

Desserts

★★

S'MORE BROWNIES

1 (21.5 oz.) package **Brownie Mix**
6 **Graham Crackers**
1 1/2 cups miniature **Marshmallows**
8 (1.5 oz) bars **Milk Chocolate**, coarsely chopped

Preheat oven to 350 degrees. Prepare brownie mix according to package directions. Spread into greased 9x13 pan. In a medium bowl, break graham crackers into 1 inch pieces and toss with miniature marshmallows and milk chocolate. Set s'more mixture aside. Bake brownies for 15 minutes in the preheated oven. Remove and sprinkle the s'more goodies evenly over the top. Bake for an additional 15 to 20 minutes, or until a toothpick inserted in the center comes out clean. Allow brownies to cool before cutting into squares.

THREE SHERBET COOLER

1/2 pint **Orange Sherbet**
1/2 pint **Lime Sherbet**
1/2 pint **Raspberry** or **Strawberry Sherbet**
Bottled **Raspberry Topping** (Melba Sauce)

Fill 4 parfait glasses with layers of the three sherbets. Top with raspberry sauce.

Desserts

★★

SNICKERDOODLES

1 cup **Shortening, Butter or Margarine**
1 1/2 cup **Granulated Sugar**
2 **Eggs**
2 3/4 cup **Flour**
2 tsp. **Cream of Tarter**
1 tsp. **Baking Soda**
1/2 tsp. **Salt**

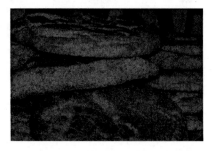

Cookie Topping:
2 tbsp. granulated **Sugar**
2 tsp. **Cinnamon**

Preheat oven to 400 degrees. With electric mixer, thoroughly cream shortening, sugar and eggs. Combine cream of tarter, baking soda and salt and blend into shortening mixture. Chill dough an hour or so in refrigerator. (Makes dough easier to handle.) Once chilled, roll into walnut-size balls. Roll balls in sugar and cinnamon mixture and place about two inches apart on ungreased cookie sheet. Bake as directed until lightly browned but still soft. (Cookies will appear puffy at first, then flatten with "crinkled" tops.)

Desserts

★★★

SUPER PEANUT BUTTER COOKIES

2 1/4 cup **Flour**
1 tsp. **Baking Soda**
1 tsp. **Salt**
1 cup **Butter, Margarine or Shortening**
3/4 cup **Brown Sugar**
3/4 cup **Granulated Sugar**
1/4 cup **Milk... Cream** if available
3/4 cup **Chunky Peanut Butter**
1 **Egg**
1 tsp. **Vanilla**
1 cup quick **Oatmeal**
1/2 cup chopped **Walnuts**
1/2 cup **Raisins**

Preheat oven to 375 degrees. Sift together flour, baking soda and salt; set aside. Using electric mixer, cream butter, brown and granulated sugar and milk. Add peanut butter, egg and vanilla; blend well. Add sifted dry ingredients and mix thoroughly. Fold in oatmeal, walnuts and raisins. Spoon onto sprayed or waxed paper-lined cookie sheets. Dough should be easy to work with. Bake until golden on edges.

Beverages

Ultimate Hot Chocolate

Hot Milk Posset

Mulled Cranberry-Apple Cider

Traditional Spiced Mulled Wine

Lemon Pear Nectar

Apple Cranberry Cooler

Orange Surprise

Citrus Cooler

Summer Sangria

Blackberry Lemonade

Beverages

****

ULTIMATE HOT CHOCOLATE

1/2 cup **Semi-Sweet Real Chocolate Chips**
1/2 cup **Sugar**
1/2 cup **Water**
Pinch of **Salt**
5 1/2 cups **Milk**
2 cups **Whipping Cream**
2 tsps. **Vanilla**
Sweetened **Whipped Cream**

Optional: grated Chocolate, grated Orange Peel, Cinnamon, Nutmeg

In a 3 quart saucepan melt chocolate chips over low heat, stirring constantly. Stir in sugar, water and salt. Cook over medium heat, stirring constantly with a wire whisk, until the mixture comes to a full boil (4 to 5 min.) boil, stirring constantly (2 min.) Stir in milk and whipping cream. Continue cooking over medium heat, stirring occasionally, until heated through (12 to 15 min.) DO NOT BOIL. Add vanilla. Beat with wire whisk or rotary beater until frothy. Pour into mugs. Top each serving with a dollop of sweetened whipping cream. If desired, garnish with any of the item listed under "optional".

Beverages

****

HOT MILK POSSET

1/8 tsp. **Almond Extract**
1 pint **Milk**
1/2 tsp. grated **Lemon Peel**
1/4 cup **Sugar**
1 **Egg White**
1/4 cup **Dark Rum**
1/2 cup **Brandy**

Heat in a saucepan the milk, lemon peel, sugar, and almond extract. When it begins to boil, beat egg white and add in. Now add rum and brandy. Serve hot.

MULLED CRANBERRY-APPLE CIDER

2 quarts (8 cups) **Apple Cider**
1 1/2 quarts (6 cups) **Cranberry Juice**
1/2 cup packed **Light Brown Sugar**
8 (3-inch) **Cinnamon Sticks** broken into pieces
10 to 15 **Whole Allspice**
20 to 25 **Whole Cloves**

Bring all ingredients to boiling. Reduce and simmer, uncovered, about 30 minutes; strain. Refrigerate cider until needed. Reheat to serve. Place a cinnamon stick stirrer in each mug, if desired. Nice served warm or well chilled.

Beverages

★★

Traditional Spiced Mulled Wine

2 bottles medium or full-bodied **Red Wine** (Bulgarian Cabernet Sauvignon is ideal)
1.5 litres **Water**
1 **Orange**, studded with 10 **Whole Cloves**
2 **Oranges** and 2 **Lemons**, sliced
6 tbsp. **Sugar** or **Honey**
5 cm **Cinnamon Stick**
2 tsp. finely grated fresh **Root Ginger**
2 tbsp **Fruit Liqueur** such as **Cointreau, Grand Manier, Calvados or Cherry Brandy**

Mix all the ingredients together in a slow cooker or a large saucepan. Heat very gently for about 20 minutes. Do not boil, or you will boil off the alcohol. Stir gently to ensure that the sugar or honey has dissolved. Serve hot or cold.

Lemon Pear Nectar

2 cups **Cold Water**
Juice of 1/2 **Lemon**
2 tbsp. **Raisins**
1 (16 oz.) can **Pears**, drained

Blend all ingredients together in a large blender. Refrigerate for 2 hours and serve over ice.

2 Servings

Beverages

****

APPLE CRANBERRY CIDER

4 quarts **Apple Juice**
2 quarts **Cranberry Juice**
1 (6 oz.) can frozen **Lemonade Concentrate**

Mix all ingredients together in a large blender. Refrigerate for 2 hours and serve over ice.

2 Servings

ORANGE SURPRISE

2 cups **Orange Juice**
1/2 cup **Water**
1/2 cup **Evaporated Milk**
Pinch of **Salt**
2 tbsp. **Powdered Sugar**
1tsp. **Almond Extract**
1/2 cup crushed **Ice**
Orange Slices

Combine ingredients and mix vigorously. Pour into chilled tall glasses. Serve with straws and a slice of orange.

3 Servings

Beverages

★★★

Citrus Cooler

3 **Black** or **Herbal Tea Bags**
1 1/2 cups **Boiling Water**
1 cup **Sugar**
1/2 cup fresh **Lemon Juice**

1/2 cup fresh **Orange Juice**
1 bottle (28 oz.) **Ginger Ale**, chilled
1 tray **Ice Cubes**
Orange Slices

Place tea bags in a large bowl. Pour boiling water over tea bags. Let stand for 5 minutes. Remove bags. Add sugar and stir until completely dissolved. Pour lemon juice, orange juice and ginger ale into tea mixture and stir briskly. Place ice cubes in a 2 quart pitcher and add tea mixture.

Serve in chilled glasses garnished with orange slices.

6 Servings

Summer Sangria

1 bottle (750 ml) **Red Wine**
1 **Orange**, peeled and squeezed
1 **Lemon**, sliced
1 **Lime**, sliced

3 tbsp. **Brandy**
1 fresh **Peach**, sliced
1/2 cup fresh **Raspberries**
1 bottle (7 oz.) **Sparkling Water**

Pour the wine into a large glass pitcher. Peel the orange in a long spiral strip. Put the peel in the wine, with one end of the spiral curled over the spout of the pitcher. Squeeze the orange, and add the juice to the wine along with the lemon and lime slices and the brandy. Refrigerate for 3 hours. Add remaining fruit one hour before serving.

Before serving, add sparkling water. Pour Sangria into tall glasses half-filled with ice cubes. If desired, add additional fruit to glasses.

Beverages

★★

BLACKBERRY LEMONADE

6 **Lemons**
2 cups **Cold Water**
1 cup **Sugar**
1/2 cup picked-over **Fresh Blackberries**
2 cups **Ice**
Lemon Slices for garnish

With a vegetable grater, remove zest from 4 lemons and squeeze enough juice from these and remaining 2 lemons to measure 1 cup.

In a saucepan, boil 1 cup water with sugar, stirring until sugar is dissolved. Add zest, lemon juice, and remaining 1 cup water and cool.

In a food processor or blender, puree blackberries and stir into lemonade. Pour blackberry lemonade through a sieve into a pitcher or other container and chill. Chill the lemonade, covered, at least until cold or up to 2 days.

Serve lemonade over ice in tall glasses, garnished with lemon slices.

Beverages

★★

*J*uicy Tips for Lovelier Lemonade

For those who don't have time to make the puckering potion from scratch, experts at Minute Maid® offer some tips on making the most out of your lemonade:

- Make sure your lemonade has real lemons (the leading powdered lemonade contains no real lemon juice)

- Look for all-natural products that provide the best-quality ingredients

- Enjoy lemonade year-round—stock up easily with cans of frozen concentrated lemonade which last for months in your freezer.

- Give a glass of lemonade and six ice cubes a whir in your blender for a real frozen-blended treat.

- Add some raspberries to your frozen-blended lemonade for an even frostier treat.

- Slice a few real lemons into a tall, iced pitcher of lemonade for a festive presentation.

- Add a splash of grape juice to your lemonade for "pink" lemonade.

- Freeze a tray of lemonade ice cubes to add special flair to sparkling water or iced tea.

- Freeze paper cups filled with lemonade and serve lemonade pops to kids.

- Enjoy a half-glass of lemonade mixed with a half-glass of iced tea—a drink known to many golfers as an "Arnold Palmer" or "half and half."

Refreshing lemonade is a versatile drink, so experiment a little! A little creativity can go a long way in creating fun and exciting drinks for family and friends to enjoy throughout the summer.

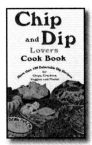

ORDER BLANK

GOLDEN WEST PUBLISHERS

☼ **5738 North Central Avenue • Phoenix, AZ 85012**

www.goldenwestpublishers.com • 1-800-521-9221 • FAX 602-234-3062

Qty	Title	Price	Amount
	Apple Lovers Cookbook	9.95	
	Arizona Cookbook	9.95	
	Bean Lovers Cookbook	9.95	
	Best Barbecue Recipes	14.95	
	Chili-Lovers' Cookbook	9.95	
	Chip and Dip Lovers Cookbook	9.95	
	Cowboy Cookbook	9.95	
	Easy Recipes for Wild Game	9.95	
	Easy RV Recipes	9.95	
	Grand Canyon Cookbook	9.95	
	Low Fat Mexican Recipes	9.95	
	New Mexico Cookbook	9.95	
	Mexican Family Favorites Cookbook	9.95	
	Peach Lovers Cookbook	9.95	
	Pecan Lovers Cookbook	9.95	
	Quick-n-Easy Mexican Recipes	9.95	
	Salsa Lovers Cookbook	9.95	
	Seafood Lovers Cookbook	9.95	
	Sedona Cookbook	9.95	
	Tequila Cookbook	9.95	
	Texas Cookbook	9.95	
	Tortilla Lovers Cookbook	9.95	
	Veggie Lovers Cookbook	9.95	

U.S. Shipping & Handling Add:
(Shipping to all other countries see website.)

1-3 Books $5.00
4+ Books $7.00

Arizona residents add 8.1% sales tax

Total $_____
(Payable in U.S. funds)

☐ My Check or Money Order Enclosed
☐ MasterCard ☐ VISA ☐ Discover ☐ American Express Verification code _____

Acct. No. _____ Exp. Date _____

Signature _____

Name _____ Phone _____

Address _____

City/State/Zip _____

Call for a FREE catalog of all our titles — Prices subject to change —